Cool Drag Racing Cars

Jon M. Fishman

Lerner Publications ◆ Minneapolis

Lerner Publications Company
A division of Lerner Publishing Group, Inc.
241 First Avenue North
Minneapolis, MN 55401 USA

For reading levels and more information, look up this title at www.lernerbooks.com.

Library of Congress Cataloging-in-Publication Data

Names: Fishman, Jon M., author.
Title: Cool drag racing cars / Jon M. Fishman.
Description: Minneapolis : Lerner Publications, [2019] | Series: Lightning bolt books. Awesome
    rides | Audience: Ages 6-9. | Audience: K to grade 3. | Includes bibliographical references and
    index.
Identifiers: LCCN 2017038555 (print) | LCCN 2017043515 (ebook) | ISBN 9781541525054 (eb
    pdf) | ISBN 9781541519947 (lb : alk. paper) | ISBN 9781541527539 (pb : alk. paper)
Subjects: LCSH: Drag racers—Juvenile literature.
Classification: LCC TL236.2 (print) | LCC TL236.2 .F57 2019 (ebook) | DDC 629.228/5—dc23

LC record available at https://lccn.loc.gov/2017038555

Manufactured in the United States of America
1-44330-34576-10/17/2017

Table of Contents

It's a Drag Racing Car!

Two drag racing cars speed down a racetrack. Their tires leave black streaks on the track. Smoke fills the air.

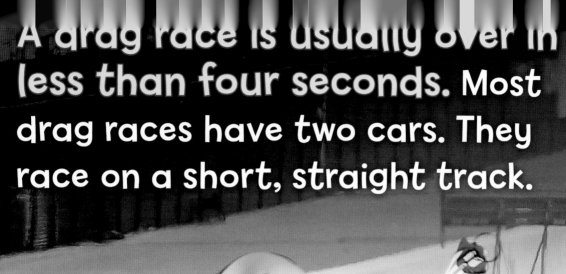

A drag race is usually over in less than four seconds. Most drag races have two cars. They race on a short, straight track.

There are two main types of drag racing cars in the United States. Top Fuel cars are long and skinny. Their engines are behind the driver.

Top Fuel cars are 25 feet (8 m) long and weigh 2,330 pounds (1,057 kg).

Funny cars are wider than Top Fuel cars. Funny car engines are in front of the driver.

The body of a funny car lifts up so the driver can climb inside.

The Drag Racing Story

People have been drag racing since the early twentieth century. The first drag races were held in large, empty places such as unused airport runways.

Drag racing was just for fun until 1951. That year, racer Wally Parks started the National Hot Rod Association (NHRA). The NHRA set up races and made rules for the sport.

Wally Parks started the NHRA to make drag racing safer.

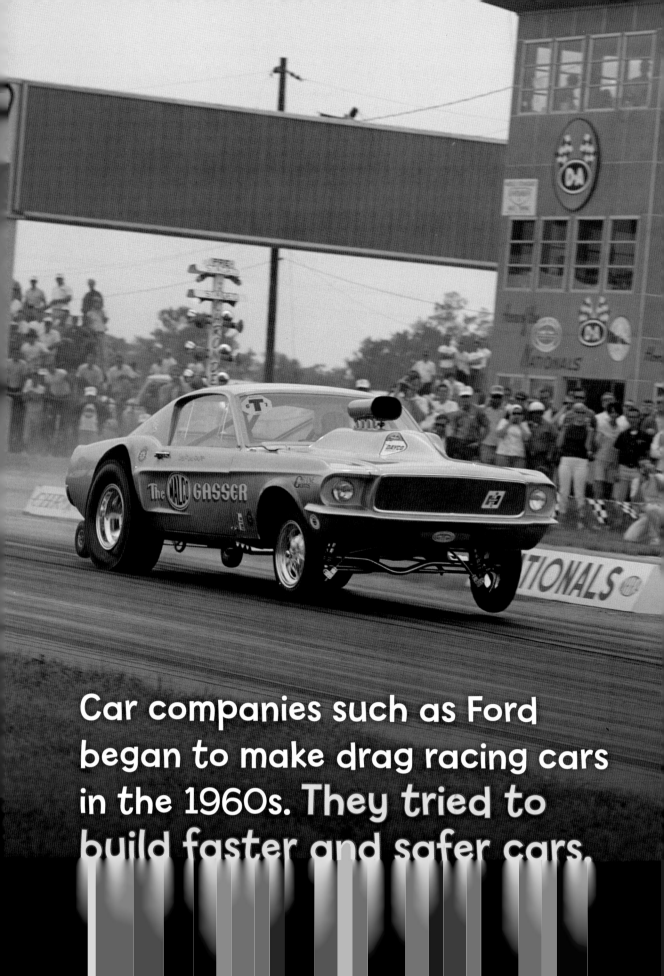

Car companies such as Ford began to make drag racing cars in the 1960s. They tried to build faster and safer cars.

Drag racing became a big business in the 1970s. Crew members began to be paid for their work. The NHRA gave prize money to the winners of drag races.

By the mid-1970s, the NHRA gave out as much as $100,000 in prize money.

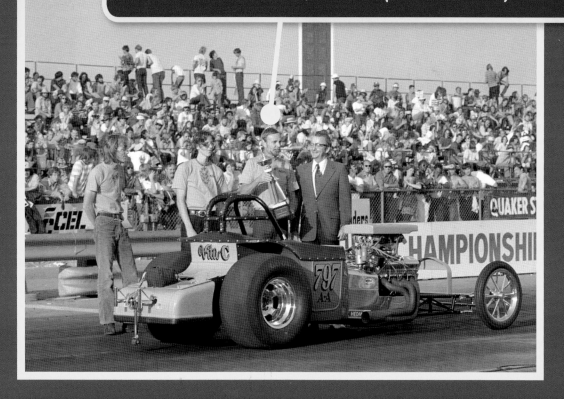

Drag Racing Car Parts

Funny cars look like cars you may see on the road. But they have differences that set them apart. That's why they're called funny cars.

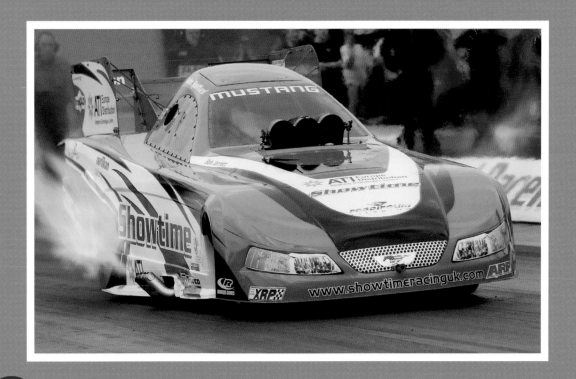

As air flows around a spoiler, it pushes the car down to keep it on the track.

Funny cars have fat tires. The back tires are slightly bigger than the front tires. A spoiler on the back of a funny car's body helps the tires grip the road.

A Top Fuel car's front tires are much smaller and skinnier than its back tires. Top Fuel cars have spoilers in the front and the back.

Top Fuel cars are the loudest cars in the NHRA.

Top Fuel cars and funny cars use the same huge engines. The engines have 10,000 horsepower. They make a lot of noise. Don't forget to bring earplugs to the racetrack!

Drag Racing Cars in Action

Vroom! A Top Fuel car roars down the track. The track is 1,000 feet (305 m) long. The car can reach the end of the track in 3.7 seconds.

Drag racing cars use two parachutes to stop at the end of a race.

Funny cars can race the same distance in 3.8 seconds. Both Top Fuel cars and funny cars can go more than 330 miles (531 km) an hour.

Motorcycles can race at up to 195 miles (314 km) an hour.

Other types of vehicles also take part in drag races. Vehicles such as motorcycles and pickup trucks streak down short tracks at amazing speeds.

Engineers work to make race cars faster and safer. They are working on drag racing engines that use electricity. Electric engines are quieter and cleaner than other engines. See you at the racetrack!

Top Fuel Car Diagram

spoiler

engine

driver

spoiler

body

front tire

back tire

Drag Racing Car Facts

- A Top Fuel car burns about 15 gallons (57 L) of fuel in a single race.

- Drag racing cars often shoot flames out of their exhaust pipes. This is because the fuel doesn't all burn up quickly enough.

- The fastest speed a person has ever reached in a car is 763 miles (1,228 km) an hour. The record was set in Nevada's Black Rock Desert in 1997.

Glossary

body: the main outside part of a car

crew member: a person such as a mechanic who works on drag racing cars

engineer: a person who designs drag racing cars and engines

funny car: a drag racing car that looks similar to regular cars on the road

horsepower: a unit that measures the power of an engine. The term *horsepower* comes from comparing the power of an engine to the power of one horse.

prize money: money given as an award for winning a drag race

runway: a straight, flat area where airplanes take off and land

spoiler: a long, narrow plate on a car that uses air to push the car to the ground

Top Fuel: a drag racing car that is long and skinny and looks similar to a rocket

Further Reading

Bach, Rachel. *The Car Race*. Mankato, MN: Amicus, 2017.

Crafts for Kids: DIY Race Cars
http://www.pbs.org/parents/crafts-for-kids/diy-race-cars/

Crane, Cody. *Race Cars*. New York: Children's Press, 2018.

Jr. Drag Racing League
http://jrdragster.nhra.com

Silverman, Buffy. *How Do Formula One Race Cars Work?* Minneapolis: Lerner Publications, 2016.

Index

Photo Acknowledgments

The images in this book are used with the permission of: Action Sports Photography/
Shutterstock.com, pp. 2, 17; Jeff Speer/Icon Sportswire/Getty Images, pp. 4, 6, 7; Brian
Bahr/Getty Images, p. 5; ISC Images & Archives/Getty Images, pp. 8, 9; Pat Brollier/The
Enthusiast Network/Getty Images, p. 10; Bud Lang/The Enthusiast Network/Getty Images,
p. 11; Michael Stokes/Shutterstock.com, pp. 12, 16; © HiroTjp/flickr.com (CC BY 2.0), p. 13;
Phillip Rubino/Shutterstock.com, pp. 14, 18; Michael Allio/Icon Sportswire/Getty Images,
p. 15, 20; Andy Cross/The Denver Post/Getty Images, p. 19; © Todd Money/flickr.com (CC
BY 2.0), p. 23..

Front cover: Marc Sanchez/Icon Sportswire/Getty Images.

Main body text set in Billy Infant regular 28/36. Typeface provided by SparkType.